man love...

memories of growing up male in rural america

poems by john clark vincent

Cover and interior design by Lisa D. Holmes (Yulan Studio, yulanstudio.com)

Published in Portland, Oregon by Yulan Studio, Inc.
Printed in the United States.

First edition
ISBN: 978-0-9915382-6-3

… for my father

table of contents

acknowledgements 7

seed wheat 9
building a gate 10
flood waters 11
farm dog 12
under the mulberry 14
picking beans 15
squirrel hunt 16
the things we do 17
pig pen 18
don’t think twice 19
taking infield 20
pure stink 21
family hour 22
burn marks 23
broken promise 24
pitching practice 25
reparations 26
heavy handed 27
my brother’s wife 28
baby bunny 29
farm aid 30
an open heart 31
man love 32
arkansas river roads 33

acknowledgements

arkansas river roads was awarded a first place prize in the 2015 oregon poetry association competition and was first published in *verseweavers*

baby bunny was previously published by *crack the spine*

family hour was previously published by *blue lake review*

my brother's wife was awarded second place in the 2011 kay snow poetry competition

seed wheat

my earliest memory begins with
me standing on a hundred-pound gunny sack
filled with seed wheat

the wheat was hard red winter wheat
bread wheat
and the sacks lined the wall
of the granary on the farm where
my father and i were born

there was a gap in that row of seed sacks
no more than a foot or two
but when you're three or four
that's a nervy jump

my older brother made it but
not me... not quite
i felt my feet touch the bag and clearly
saw the galvanized metal tub just before
my forehead kissed it hard

next thing i knew, my dad was running
to the house, whistling the way only he could whistle
me under his right arm, face down
blood streaming

i remember the doctor's office and my head being taped
then sitting at my grandmother's kitchen table
watching her give some woman a permanent

they made a big deal out of my bandaged head
but i knew they weren't worried about me
as much as how that permanent was going to turn out

building a gate

when i was twelve or so
i had not yet formed a clear opinion of god
but i was certain about my dad

no stronger man had ever lived
and though he spoke in similar terms of
his father, i was too clever to be fooled

it bothered me some knowing that
i regularly let him down
but he seldom mentioned it after a job was done

he seemed okay, in fact, which starkly
contrasted with the flood of invective
he employed to fine-tune most projects i tackled

but that one day
i think it was mid-july and hot
but not yet august hot

we were building a gate that had to be built
in spite of the startling downpour of unexpected rain
and my father's focus made clear i had no other choice

but to stay and see it through
so i fought my urge to run for shelter and
took the full force of that sudden storm

i laughed, in fact, when i looked into my father's face
and saw him smiling at me
as he pulled the corner post tight

flood waters

growing up
a flood came to my house
every seven years
like clockwork
our particular river would get lonely and
roll on over for a visit

as a child i spent hours wading in
fields of water
driveways of water
sheds of water
basements of water
roads of water

dragonflies, diving beetles, water striders, frog's eggs
but i never saw a single snake

a catastrophe isn't quite so scary if
you're always looking forward to it

farm dog

we called him luke
even though our father named him lucifer
the lone remaining pup

of the litter a stray had borne
beneath the room added at the back of our house
half coyote half dog

i often wondered how it was his mother
had conceived him
what wildness had taken hold of her

and what must it be like for him
to live among the enemy
who slew his family and

would have slain him had he not
hidden himself so cleverly…
his late appearance stilled my father's hand

and somehow won his heart…
that is how luke came to be our dog
came to be the companion who, each day, ran beside our truck

for miles and played all day until
he ran beside us home again
i could feel how much he wanted to love us

how much he needed to be loved
in the ways that dogs and coyotes need love
with closeness and with distance

but distance always seemed to win
because in all those years we touched him so few times
my little brother, my mother, and once by me

one night i came home late
luke met me and nervously asked me to run my hand
through the rough hair along his lean back

it was not long after that i shot him
once through the head
with a rifle i had borrowed from a neighbor

luke's back was broken when
startled by an ill-tempered shepherd
he rolled beneath the wheels he ran beside

my younger brother was driving but
it was my job to free that desperate dog
and i was careful to do it as gently as i could

then i lifted him into the truck
we took him home
and buried him beside his favorite tree

under the mulberry

not that often but
often enough
i would walk south of our house to a mulberry

that grew alone on a sandy rise
at the eastern edge of the twenty-acres
between our farm's house and

the pasture beyond the shelter belt
where feeder pigs or yearling cattle
passed their time

it was a patient little tree
purple berries… no worms
shade for several yards of sand

and for me
when i needed more than anything
to be sheltered from the bright light of expectation

picking beans

farm life can get a little lonely so visiting
the drake family was always a high point for me
five girls and every one of them pretty

and as different from one another as
tomatoes and green beans
both of which my brothers and i would

help them pick at family get togethers...
their mother planted rows and rows of beans
which supported many winter meals

i was happy to pick those beans
tried to do my very best
to earn a chance to crank the homemade ice cream

that always followed our cookout
and to earn the admiration
of any one of those drake girls

squirrel hunt

i grew up with an admiration for hunters
and wanting to hunt myself

i watched the smooth beauty of
pointers owned by friends of my uncle

we couldn't afford such dogs but i was
grateful to have seen them work

my father was slow to allow it
but eventually i used both shotgun on birds

and rifle on rabbits and squirrels...
i don't know where the desire for squirrel came from

maybe it was my mother's side of the family
the ozark-oklahoma side

i scared off countless squirrels
until i finally hit one

watched it fall thirty feet
then try to crawl to shelter

it was dying but it wasn't dead
as i approached it with little experience

in the business of death
when it turned on its side to face me

i saw a living face
a face with eyes that had stories to tell

it was telling me one as i stood there
and it was asking for another chance

i had no opportunities to give that squirrel
so i simply cried as i killed it

then i put the guns away and
found other ambitions to fill my time

the things we do

i've always been afraid of appearing weak
of being laughed at or having anyone notice me
for what i thought might be the wrong reasons

that's why i told no one
when i was eleven and
snapped the ulna in my left arm at school

i furtively used my right hand to lift my left
onto and off of my books and tablets
i gritted my teeth as i carried my clarinet

with my broken arm
down our long driveway
so the bus driver would not suspect

then dropped it to the ground the instant
he drove away
i kicked on the front door of our house

explained to my mom that my arm was not working
and i didn't know why
then my grandmother died

so i sat with my arm on a pillow
watching my father struggle with his own hidden pain until
five days later we went to get an x-ray

i was so relieved to know
there was a good reason
i had to struggle that hard to take the pain

pig pen

a pig got out of the makeshift pen we'd
set up south of the house and my dad had
made his mind up about getting that pig back in

so i watched for a while from the back porch
then finally went inside the house when it was clear
that neither man nor pig was going to bend

it surprised me when i found my mother in tears
watching from the window
he's going to kill it she said

and i noticed he'd picked up a chunk
of timber and the pig's face was bleeding…
it had reached the point where neither

participant had any notion of what had led them there
so i left my mom, who was sobbing by then
and went to my room, wondering what i should do

don't think twice

thursday nights i would sit on
the turquoise shag carpet overlaying
a beautiful ancient oak hardwood floor

the floor that lay beneath my mother's
ornate stereo cabinet just across from her
pink upright piano that served several purposes

my mother sat in an uncomfortable blue embroidered chair
as we listened to her albums of peter paul and mary...
who would have guessed that she and i

would spend time elsewhere on these evenings
me in my world and she in hers...
in fact i sometimes wondered if anyone

understood what was going on
or if they saw us simply as two people... one sitting
on the floor and the other eating sandwiches

taking infield

god i loved taking infield as a kid
leather on my hand
dust rising from kicked dirt

looking for how it
comes off the bat
jumping up or racing through

playing the hop
accepting the ball then
letting it go

couldn’t hit for shit
and games were just okay
but i could take infield all day long

pure stink

the day was august hot
the kind of heat that comes long
after any hope of cool breezes or
summer storms

the heat of acceptance
the heat of just doing whatever
comes next

and next meant burying the pig
that died several days ago

died in the passageway between
the corral and the
young cottonwoods we fenced
early in the year

i think my dad was in a bad
mood or maybe just mad at me
when he asked me
why hadn't i buried that pig yet
why had i let it lay in that heat for
several days now

how's that my job i thought but didn't ask
instead i found a shovel and
walked as slowly as i could toward
a job i didn't want to do

the reality i discovered was worse than
i expected

i refuse to put you through it
the way only half the pig rolled over
the infinity of maggots
the gagging stench

there's no reason for you to have to
go there

family hour

my mom and dad spent the majority
of their lives arguing
sometimes bitterly, always angrily

of course there were lulls
the occasional oasis
promising sweetness and cool opportunities

but more often than not those oases
turned out to be illusions born of need
and briefly sustained through sheer grit

to this day i do not understand
why they stayed together
though at the time i wanted them to

especially when the day finally arrived and
my mother announced she was leaving
she sat on a stiff, nice looking blue chair by the window

as my dad lay on the couch with his arm
drawn up across his forehead, face turned away...
my two brothers and i were spread around the room

as my mother laid out the reasons she was going
and my dad admitted he had made mistakes
then my mom surprised me

she asked my little brother if she should stay or go
she put it on him to decide...
she shouldn't have asked, and she shouldn't have stayed

burn marks

my grandfather august was a short and somewhat fat
german man with a forehead twice as high as it
would have been had he combed his hair differently

he rolled prince albert into loose fat cigarettes that
marked his seat wherever it was with a halo of spilled tobacco
his fingers burned black from falling asleep with

these treasures still glowing between them
he used to pimp my grandmother mercilessly then
wink at me when she lit into him

and he was at our kitchen table the day my father
chose to expound on a notion that recently had come to him
that children owed a debt of gratitude

to their parents simply for being born
i listened to my dad's bullshit all the way through
then glanced at august before responding

gee dad i said
thanks for screwing mom
then didn't breathe till august started laughing

broken promise

there was a kid i knew briefly in high school
you don't need to know his name
but he died as an underclassman like

so many young people do
in a car with an open container
passenger to a classmate in the midst of a lesson

i mention him because it was at his funeral
as i looked into his casket while leaving the church
i began to sob uncontrollably

don't honestly know why
maybe i hadn't recognized death before that moment
or maybe never felt that vulnerable

i was with my dad because my brother was
pall bearing and my mom was at home
with my kid brother and new baby sister

dad didn't know quite what to do with me
so we sat quietly in the car for most of the graveside service
but eventually we got to talking

i told my dad that i wanted to make a deal with him
i wanted him to agree that when he or i died
the other one wouldn't cry

he thought about that a bit then looked away
i'll agree to it he said
but i imagine i'll cry anyway

pitching practice

i never expected my older brother
to teach my sons anything significant
when i took them for a rare weekend visit

but the love of sports he shared
with my younger boy pulled them out
to the yard where i once played

and where on this weekend the fork ball
passed to a new generation
i was glad it happened that way

but never imagined my boy
would throw that pitch for the final strike
in a hard fought season ending game

i yelled for him to throw it and
my stomach dropped nearly as much
as that pitch did

he loved winning that game but me
i love the story it told about
an older brother i never fully knew

reparations

three years after making my decision
i told my wife i was leaving...
it took that long to hold my fear down

i managed to get some clothes into the car
but had not sufficiently thought through
the harder job

the race through rooms
the search for two frightened children
the need to throw a line

across an impossible distance
a reach i hadn't realized
i would not be able to make

i found them separately
rigid with worry they believed they
were not showing

angry and cool and white-knuckled
fighting for a foothold
as every heart in every room shattered

i think i promised i'd be back
i must have said at least that much
before i left

but whatever words were spoken
any lines that lived were cut
and four boats were set adrift

we all survived
knowing reparations were in order
even if we weren't sure what reparations are

heavy handed

i didn't see my older brother
much after my first two years
of college

he gave up trying to run my life
and i gave up letting him try…
it was a mutual decision

but sometime between that parting
and middle age
he ran out of 'want to'

life was too much of an uphill climb
he was a puncher and i guess
he just punched himself out

he didn't have anything left
so he focused on trying to go
the distance but he got sick

and he got slower and slower
at coming off his stool until
one day he decided to stay put

the fight was actually called
long before he left the ring
but eventually it was time to go

so i went to see him one last time
asked him what he'd like
which turned out to be a bottle of single malt scotch

i got him the best fifth i could find
in that small town
and sat with him as he savored a glass

my brother's wife

my brother's wife is happy again

she walks, she laughs
her weight is down
she even found a job

she's been to texas seven times
to see her daughters and their kids

she flew to phoenix just last month

the world's her oyster once again
and shucked though it may have been
she remembers what it means to be a pearl

my brother's wife is happy again

and i'm not saying the dullness or the darkness
she used to carry with her was my brother's fault alone

but since he died
her petals one by one have simply just unfurled

baby bunny

both my sons were waiting
sitting on the step when i pulled up
a rare beginning to my alternating weekend

they were not smiling
and though anger was common between them
i sensed none of that today

there was a rabbit they said
a baby caught by their new dog
the one they were learning to love

is it dead i asked
we think it's hurt real bad
we tried to make him stop you know

they were my children
not knowing what to do
yet believing that their father would

it's not your fault i said
wait here and i'll go look
and hoped with every step to find it dead

finding instead a body barely breathing
eyes closed
so tiny and so torn

knowing what had to happen
i scanned the yard for any helpful tool
remembered at last my father's axe

still sitting in my ex-wife's garage
i retrieved it and i used it
then wrapped the baby's body in a paper towel

my sons were in the car when i returned
stealing glances as i took my seat
doing my best to hide my tears

farm aid

as my dad aged he got philosophical
no one can own the earth he'd say
it's just not right

other times he was deeply nostalgic
collecting old harness and brass beds at farm sales
as one family farm after another went down

he seemed to sense he was arriving at the end of
more than just his own life
he was marking the end of generations of hard hope

and he was doing it alone
he even moved to the basement to sleep in
the space my older brother and i once shared

where i had painted a peace sign on the concrete
and where he now roughed in studs to create a room
that he would never finish

he grew a beard in defiance of those who
tried to shame my long hair
and he did his best to make peace with himself...

i wish i could tell you this story ends well
and that this man who would fight anyone anytime
yet find sweet joy in a field of sprouting seed

would end his days happy
but the stroke sealed the deal
and his last ten years were really hard to see

an open heart

my little brother has been bigger than me
for more than fifty years now
tougher too

he's walked a hard path in a hard way
very little jail time and that's
probably due more to luck than i want to know

but now
after a lifetime of swapping stories across
a backyard fence we never found our way around

i wonder if i will outlast him
as i picture him on the surgeon's table
chest split and heart open

i want to be there
i want each tear i give up to
fall upon his fading hopes

i want to take his heart in my hands
and shake it and slap it and
kiss it and hug it and tuck it in

i want it to sleep soundly and dream
good honest simple dreams
i want it to awaken and remember me when i'm gone

man love

i believe my dad wanted to love my brothers and me
just as i want to love my sons and
they in turn have sought to love in their own ways

but how does one man love another
how do we know when we've
done enough or learned to care enough

that our caring qualifies as love
who defines that
who grades the effort or

understands that the larger part of man love
is showing how to take a punch
and still remain a decent human being

my dad is gone now
my sons have moved away
and as i sit and wonder how we've scored

i want to believe it's love i feel
when i think of all the pain
we've divided so equally among us

arkansas river roads

these are the roads i walked when i was young
loose sand
running along fields of wheat

edged with the white bark of dead cottonwood
rising like totems to even harder times
from the weeds and scrub too smart
to be plowed under

i didn't hike these roads for pleasure
i walked them to do a job
to get from here to over there

but that doesn't mean i didn't dream
didn't feel the sand making a place for me

hinting as it rolled beneath my boots that
it was my sand and the rough grass
that grew through it was my grass

i remember the taste of it
the endless need for hope and tough hands
and the wistful way it settled in each evening

www.ingramcontent.com/pod-product-compliance
Lightning Source LLC
Chambersburg PA
CBHW032011120726
47902CB00014B/2088

* 9 7 8 0 9 9 1 5 3 8 2 6 3 *